12 Habit Holding You Back From Success.

Habits we need to drop to be successful

By

Bella Judith

Table of content

- **Critical Things You Need For Life Success**

Conclusion.

Introduction

People believe that success comes from outside sources. They believe that successful people worked hard to earn more money, but this is only half the story. The other half is that successful people do more than just work long hours at the office. They are avoiding bad habits that would hinder their success.

Their external success is the result of both external and internal hard work.

Internal work includes the difficult question, "Do I have the same habits as a successful person?"

If you can imagine a seven-figure entrepreneur spending their day exactly as you do, you're on the right track. If you can't, you've discovered your problem. You are requesting success without becoming the person who achieves that level of success.

Successful people do not break their promises, do not eat fast food, and do not blame others for their misfortunes.

chapter 1

Putting off Important Tasks

Everyone procrastinates at some point in their lives. The important thing is to determine whether your procrastination is simply putting off a task to take a much-needed break or if it is a chronic problem that affects your work.

If your procrastination causes you to produce subpar work. If your boss, family, friends, or coworkers criticize your procrastination. Or if you know it has a negative impact on your work. Your procrastination is a problem, and you will have to address it.

Chapter 2

Budget Overspending and Exceeding

Are you always in debt? Feels like your bills are getting bigger and bigger. Credit cards out of hand? Do you have a mountain of debt on your chest?
If any of these apply to you, you may have a spending problem and should either earn more or spend less. The steps to spending less money are simple, but few people take the time or make the effort to follow them.

The good spending habits

- Create a budget.
- Make a budget for yourself and stick to it.
- Don't bring your credit cards.
- You do not require everything you desire.
- Avoid shopping with overspending friends.
- Pay your bills first, then save the rest.

Chapter 3

Mindless Entertainment Addiction Holds You Back

I'll be honest: this is one of my current bad habits. I work hard and keep myself mostly on the straight and narrow when it comes to habits, so I allow myself to read for pure pleasure.

As long as it is kept to a minimum, there is nothing wrong with it. If I couldn't read a book like Ready Player One or Girl on the Train on occasion. I'd go insane. However, when you jeopardize your work or your life, you must deal with it.

Chapter 4

Spending Excessive Time on Social Media

Social media has become as addictive as that first cup of coffee in the morning. Many people are left wanting more after receiving a temporary gratification from the number of "likes" and views on the pictures and videos they post.
Not only does social media prevent us from forming meaningful long-term relationships, but we are also competing to see who has the "best life."

Effect of spending too much time on social media

- Anxiety has been linked to social media.
- Contributes to low self-esteem.
- People's lives are frequently compared to those on social media, which can lead to depression.
- Stop looking at other people's lives and start living your own.

- We neglect spending quality time with those around us.

If you find it difficult to give up social media, try reducing the number of hours you spend on it and see how your life improves.

Chapter 5

Accepting "Yes" from Everyone

We're all guilty of saying yes when we really want to say no to things and people. We sometimes take on more than we can handle because we are afraid of being judged or disliked.

Even when we try to convince ourselves that we will not say yes again, we become scared, tense, and ultimately say yes.

Because we all want to be liked, we are afraid of being rejected or coming across as unkind and rude.

Saying no doesn't make you a bad person; rather, it just means you made the decision not to spend your time on activities you don't enjoy.

Chapter 6

Multitasking Reduces Productivity.

Everyone aspires to increase productivity by putting out more work quickly. Even some job specifications list it as a "must" to be taken into consideration for the position.

Numerous studies have shown, however, that the human brain is not capable of multitasking effectively. You are merely switching your attention from one task to another while attempting to finish the two quickly.

It has been established that juggling multiple tasks causes more mistakes than it solves.

Causes of multitasking

- causes tension
- causes fear
- We now use it as justification for taking on more responsibilities than we'd like.

According to science, humans are incapable of efficiently performing two tasks.

Chapter 7
Concentrating On Negative Thoughts

In order to protect ourselves from the unknown, we create negative scenarios in our minds. This is the basis of negative thinking.
As a means of being "safe," this style of thinking prevents us from developing and from taking chances in life.
You must alter your way of thinking if you want to transform your life.

How to change your thinking

- Don't let pessimistic thoughts impair your judgment.
- Thinking negatively prevents you from developing.
- Practice thinking good ideas instead of negative ones.
- Before beginning your day every morning, listen to something uplifting.
- Get rid of the people that think negatively.
- Depression results from negativity.

Chapter 8

Being Late.

The real reason most of us are late everywhere is that we simply do not want to be early. We don't bother making the extra effort required to be on time because it isn't important to us. We know deep down that the people who are expecting us will forgive or dismiss our tardiness.

Would you be late if someone promised you a million dollars and all you had to do was meet them the next day at the address they provided? It all comes down to priorities and the adage "we make time for things we want."

How to avoid being late

- Being late is considered disrespectful.
- Attend your appointments on time.
- Allow enough time for you to prepare for appointments.
- Set reminders and alarms to help you avoid being late.

Chapter 9

Stress Eating Prevents Progress.

It has become common practice for many of us to utilize food as a coping technique to deal with stress, boredom, and loneliness.
It's critical to distinguish between physical hunger and emotional feeding requests. Because the feelings that made you hungry will still be there after you eat the calories, emotional hunger shouldn't be sated.
Understanding that food is for fuel and not for consolation will help you find healthier ways to deal with your emotions.

How to deal with your emotions

- Stay away from guilt
- Don't "Should," but rather DO

The decision to be lazy is one you make every day. Make the alternative and get up.
Spend less time with your buddies if you find them to be slackers. We are influenced by friends, often without realizing it.

Chapter 10

Your Progress Is Being Impeded By Your Jealousy Of Others.

In one way or another, we have all been envious of others' possessions, vacations we can't take, or romantic relationships we can't have.
Being envious of those who are luckier than you is pointless because it doesn't change anything.
You won't achieve anything by snarling and gritting your teeth while you watch others win.

Don't waste your time being jealous

- Don't be envious of others just because they appear to be luckier than you.
- Find a means to get something you want if someone else already has it.
- Jealousy just fosters resentment.
- Continual thinking
- Insecurity
- Time wastage

Chapter 11

Taking On More Than You Can Handle Is Preventing You From Moving Forward

When you have the "disease to please," you frequently respond "yes" to requests without first considering how you'll carry them out.
The cost we pay to avoid rejection, to feel incomparable, or to stay busy may not always be justified by the benefit.
Delaying time with loved ones so you may complete one more project at work will have long-term consequences. You cannot take on so much without it affecting other aspects of your life.
It's critical to consider the benefits and hazards of devoting your time to yet another work.

How to stop taking more than you can handle

- Give up assisting others with their issues
- Avoid adding more task to your already packed schedule.
- Never work nonstop.

- Spend some time alone.
- Unwind more.

Saying no to repeated requests for assistance is one of the most difficult things to do. But you have to take action. It is simple to become bogged down to the point where you achieve nothing when you continuously take on new jobs and assist others with their work.

chapter 12

Being Distracted Is Preventing You From Advancing.

At the moment, we would rather leave the house without shoes than allow ourselves to leave our phones at home.
The primary source of distraction for most people when they open their eyes in the morning is their phone. It's become routine to check our emails right away, browse social media for the newest updates, or send SMS to let others know you're important.

How to get less distracted

- Work on your focus and focus on one thing at a time.
- When pursuing a goal, bear in mind the destination.
- Take distractions away
- Shut off your phone.
- Study time management.
- Check email less often
- Disable notifications

Critical Things You Need For Life Success

Belief

Your success depends on even just having the belief that you can succeed. If all you are filled with is self-doubt, you cannot give your best. If you want to have a shot of success, you must have faith in both yourself and your aspirations. Nothing can stop you if your heart and head are both 100 percent sure that you can succeed. You can reach any height and fulfill all of your desires. Just have faith.

Action.

Belief alone is insufficient. You must take constant action in its wake. To acquire concentration, take the initiative and create a clear plan of action. To succeed and fulfill your goals, fully implement those plans. Recall that until you move, nothing changes.

Discipline.

The mere act of acting is insufficient. To succeed, you need discipline. Having self-control over instinctual desires, such as instant gratification, requires discipline in both thought and action. Making excuses for improper or insufficient execution of your strategies and plans for success is not being disciplined. Asserting your willpower to succeed is what discipline is.

Effort.

The virtues of effort and hard labor are unquestionable. Even if you put in the time and effort to learn and comprehend something, even if you don't have all the answers, you are already ahead of the game. Those who work hard and with dedication will succeed.

Persistence.

The most successful people are those who are steadfast in their beliefs and practices. Even when things aren't going their way, they stick to their primary goals and objectives. They stay focused and committed to their goals because they believe in them. If what you are doing or working for is vital to you, you will see it through to the conclusion. Persistence, patience, and practice are required for success.

Attitude.

A reasonable, positive attitude is the correct attitude. A reasonable, positive attitude fosters optimism, confidence, and true friendships. These things propel people through the worst of life's storms and bring them safely to shore. If you can think positively and behave positively, you will achieve amazing things. Your attitude influences your altitude.

Sacrifice.

Sacrifice is necessary for success. On the road to success, you must be willing to make some compromises. For instance, you will have to give up some personal time to complete important tasks. In a similar vein, you will have to give up some of your comfort in order to fully commit to your goals. "No pain; no gain" is applicable here, as it is in most situations in life.

Creativity.

Even though it can't guarantee success on its own, creativity is a crucial component of success. You can perform dynamically and solve problems intuitively by using your creative ability, talents, and skills. To establish your authority in your field of work, tune into the limitless intelligence of your creative spirit and talents. The only thing that can make you stand out from the competitors, ensure your survival, and lead to long-term success is your originality.

Gratitude.

Genuine success originates in a state of gratitude. Says Melody Beattie

"Gratitude opens the door to life's fullness. It makes what we already have more than enough. Denial is transformed into acceptance, disorder into order, and obscurity into clarity. A meal may become a feast, a house can become a home, and a stranger can become a friend thanks to it. Gratitude clarifies our past, offers comfort to the present, and inspires a vision for the future.

If you ever do succeed, keep in mind that being grateful is the icing on the cake!

Conclusion

The only way to make yourself to achieve your life goals is to begin. Make no more excuses. Stop putting yourself down. Simply begin.

www.ingramcontent.com/pod-product-compliance
Lightning Source LLC
LaVergne TN
LVHW030124160826
845673LV00019B/3012

* 9 7 9 8 8 4 6 2 9 5 6 9 8 *